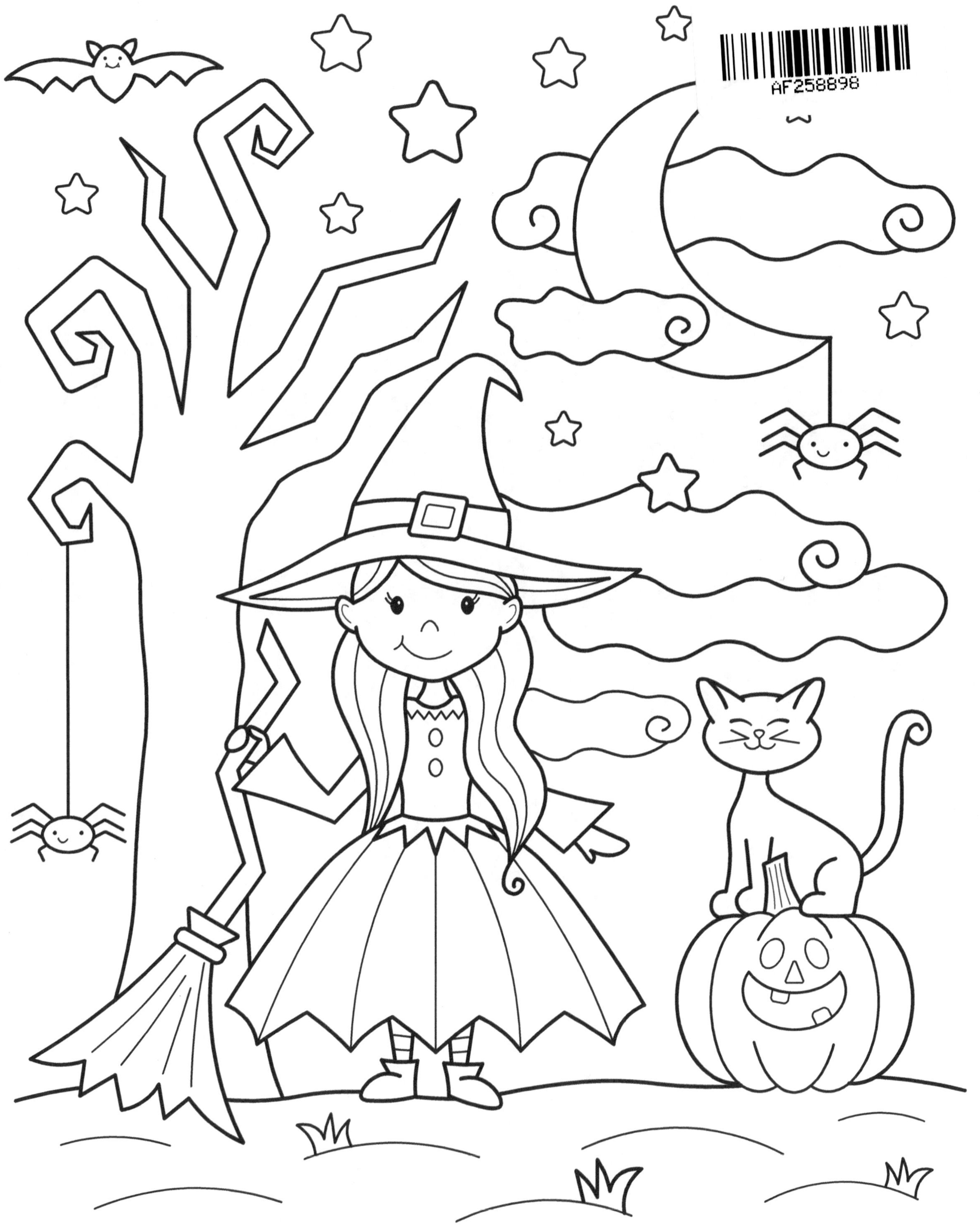
AF258898

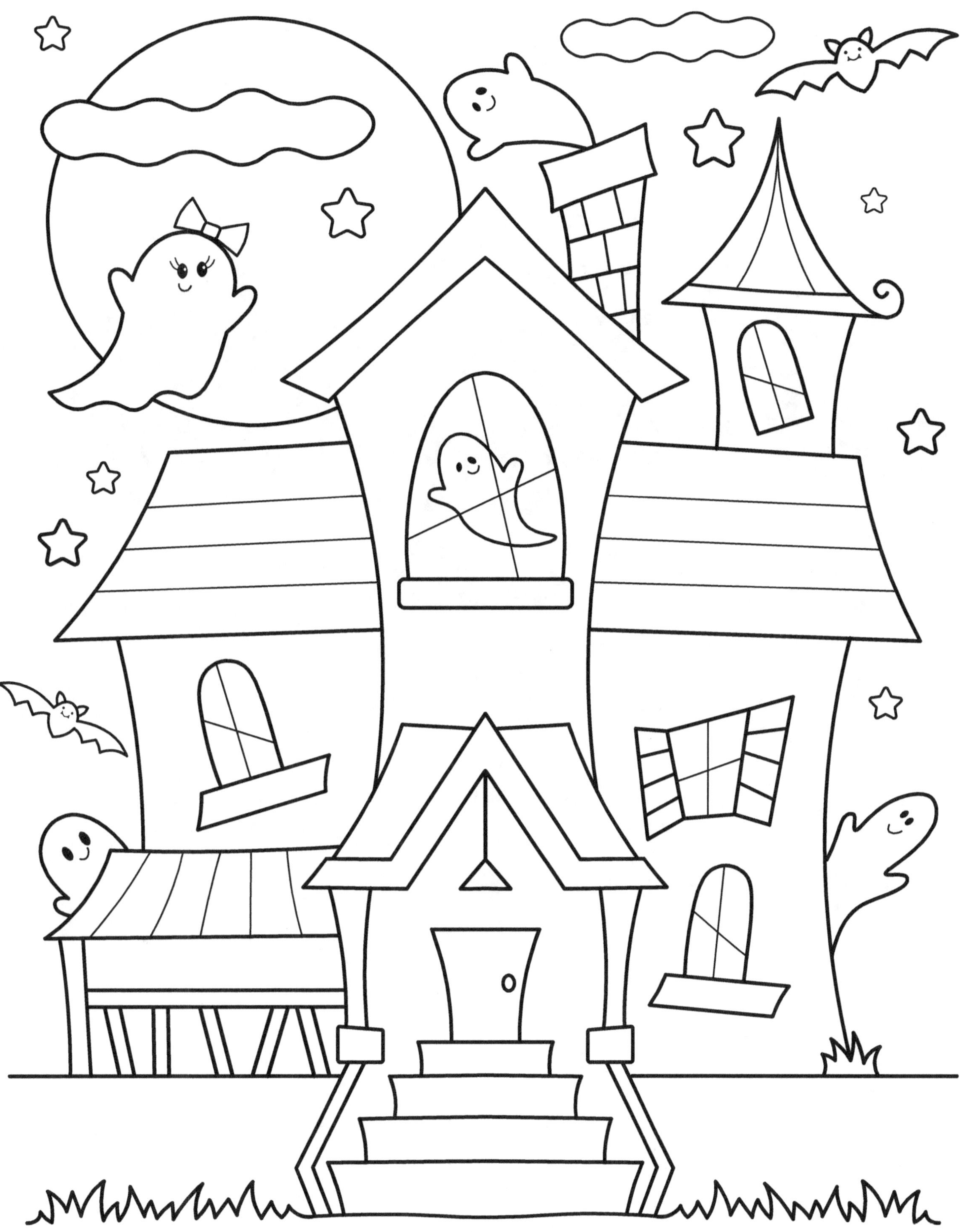

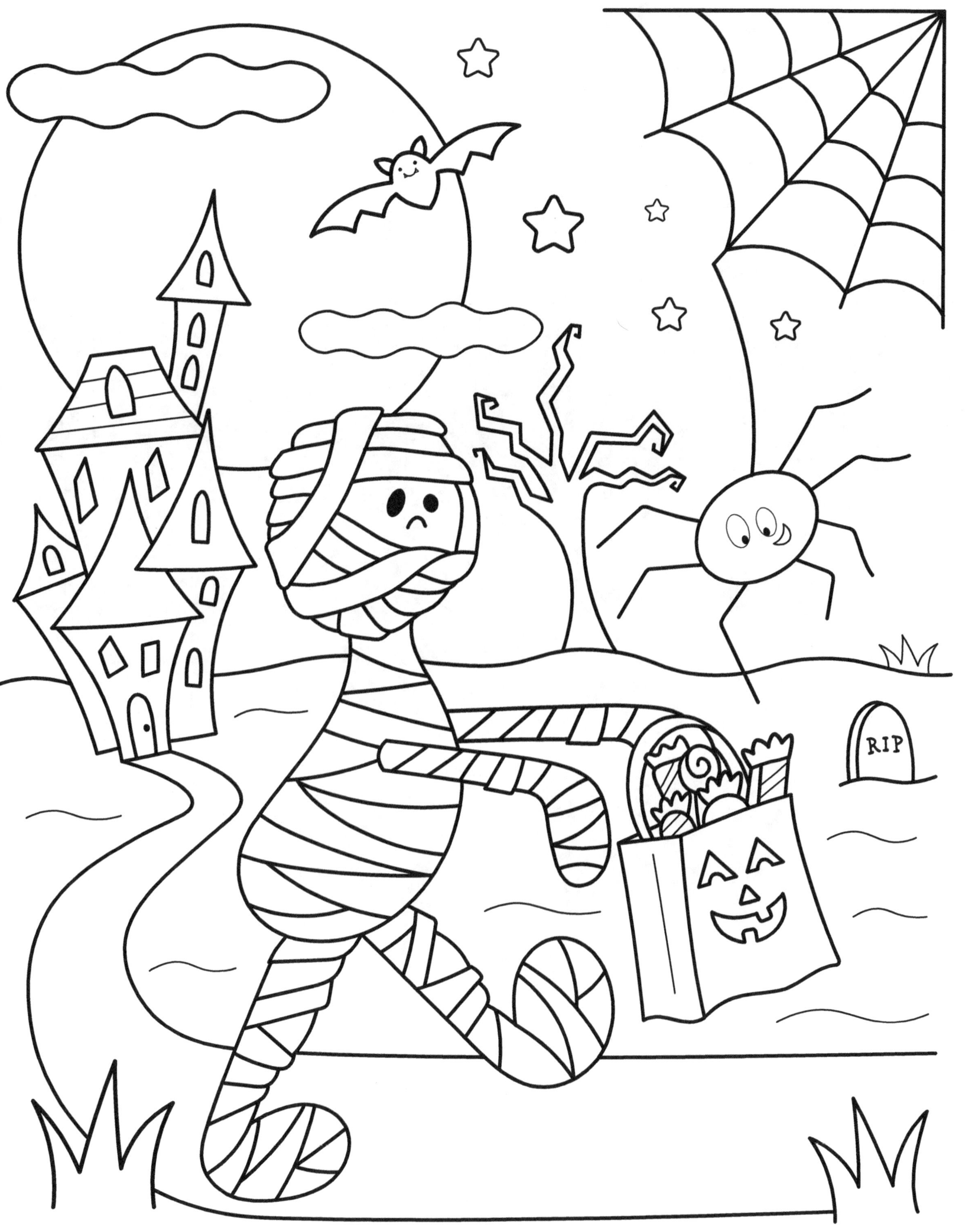
RIP

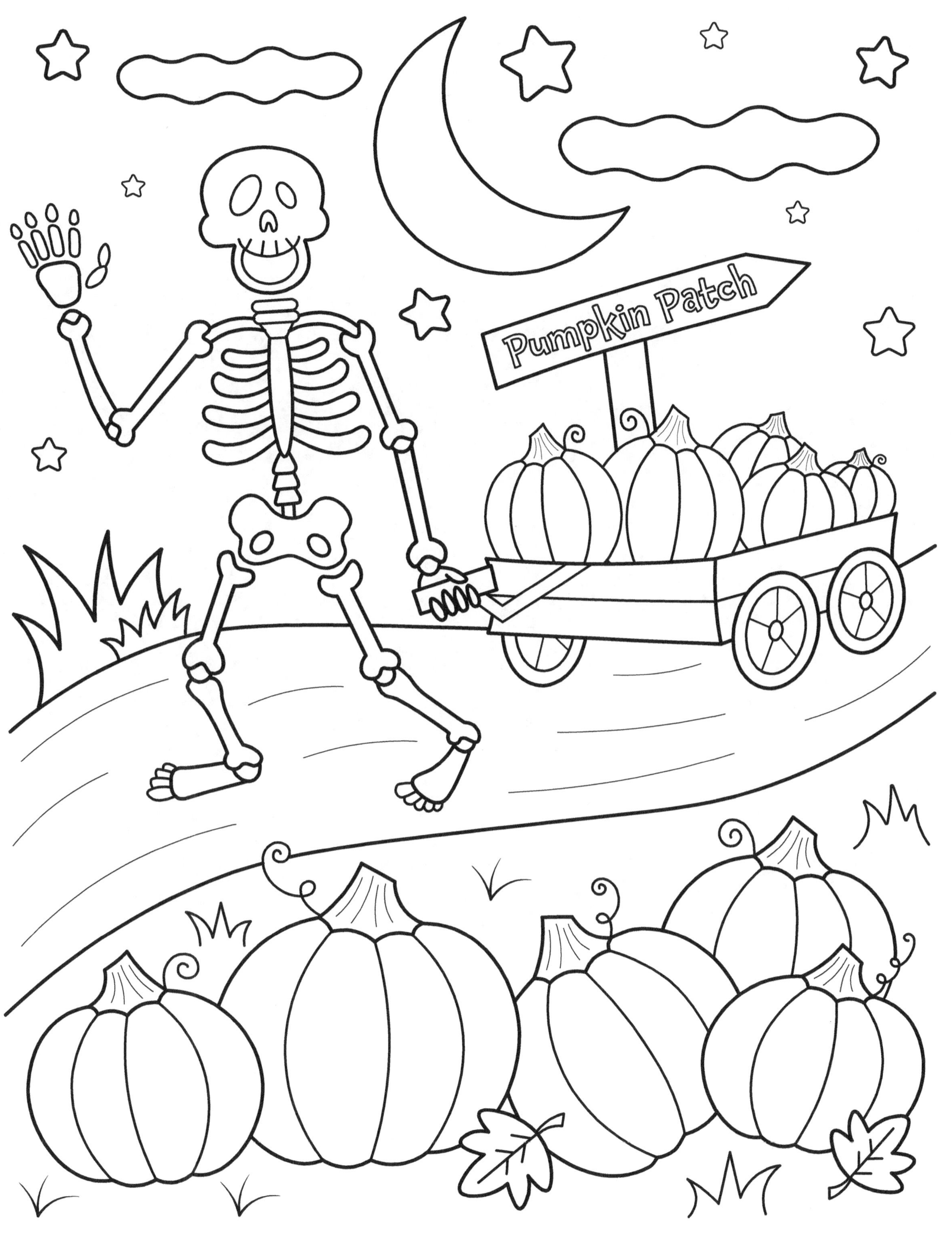
Pumpkin Patch

Can you help the pumpkin find the pumpkin patch?

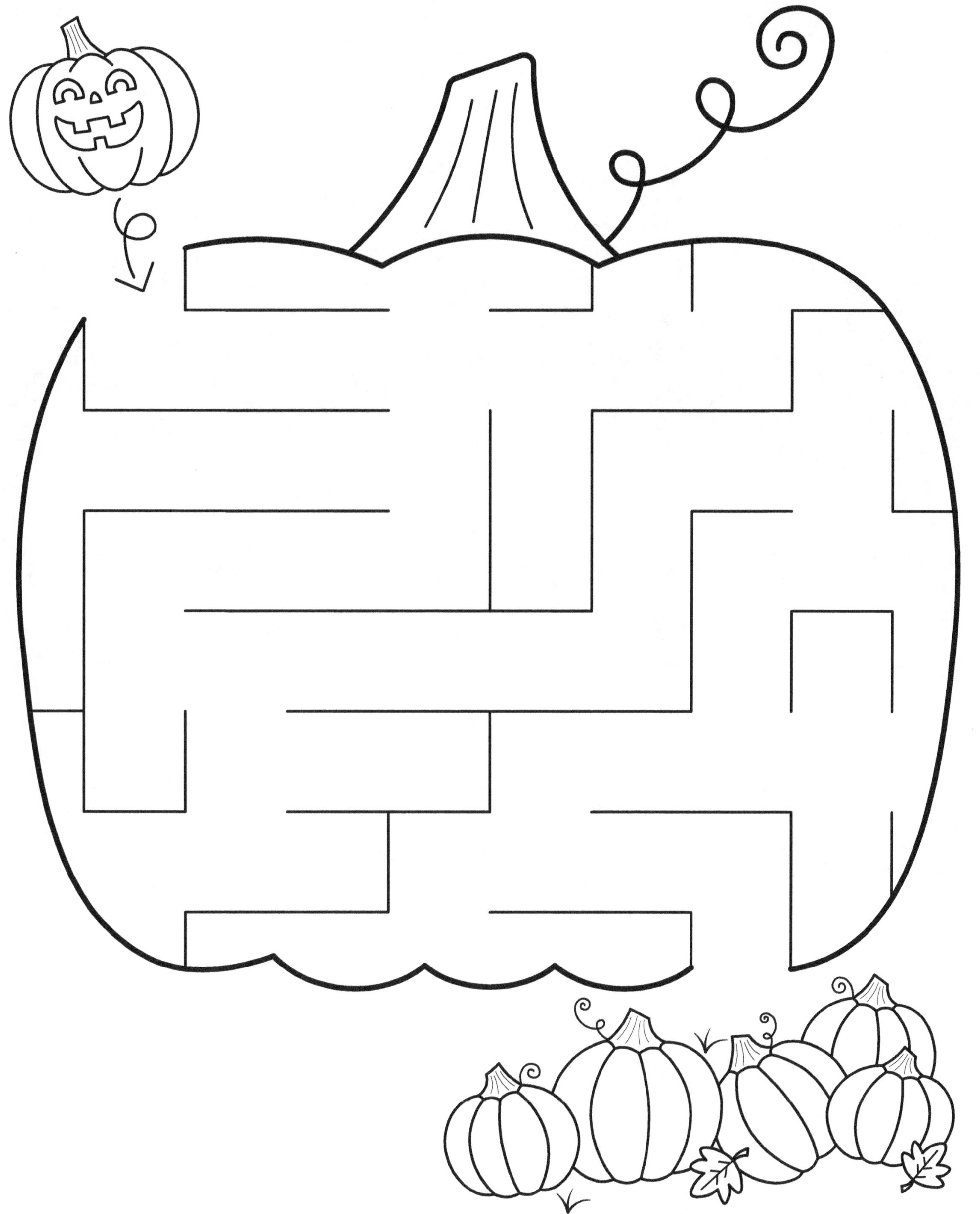

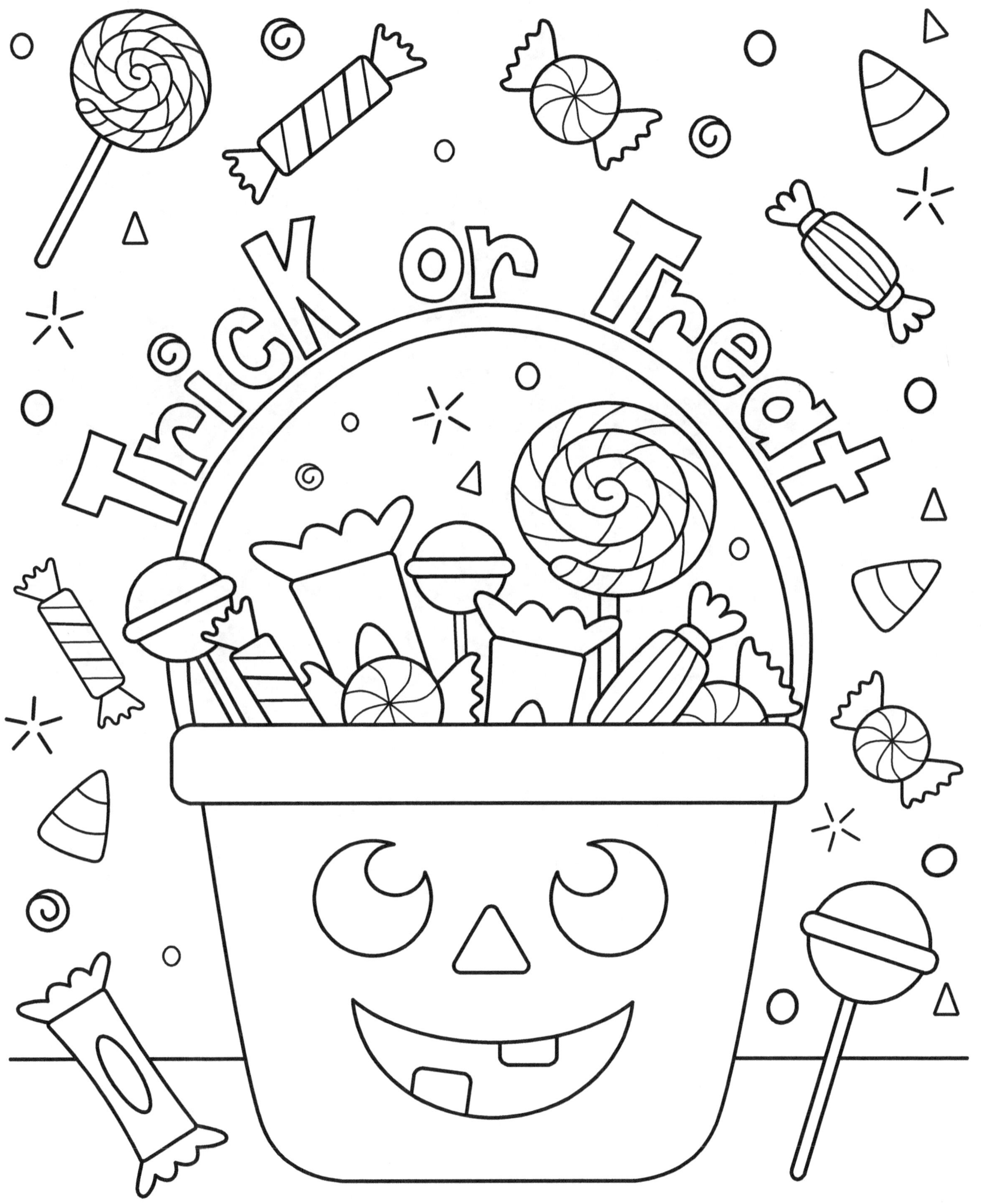

Trick or Treat

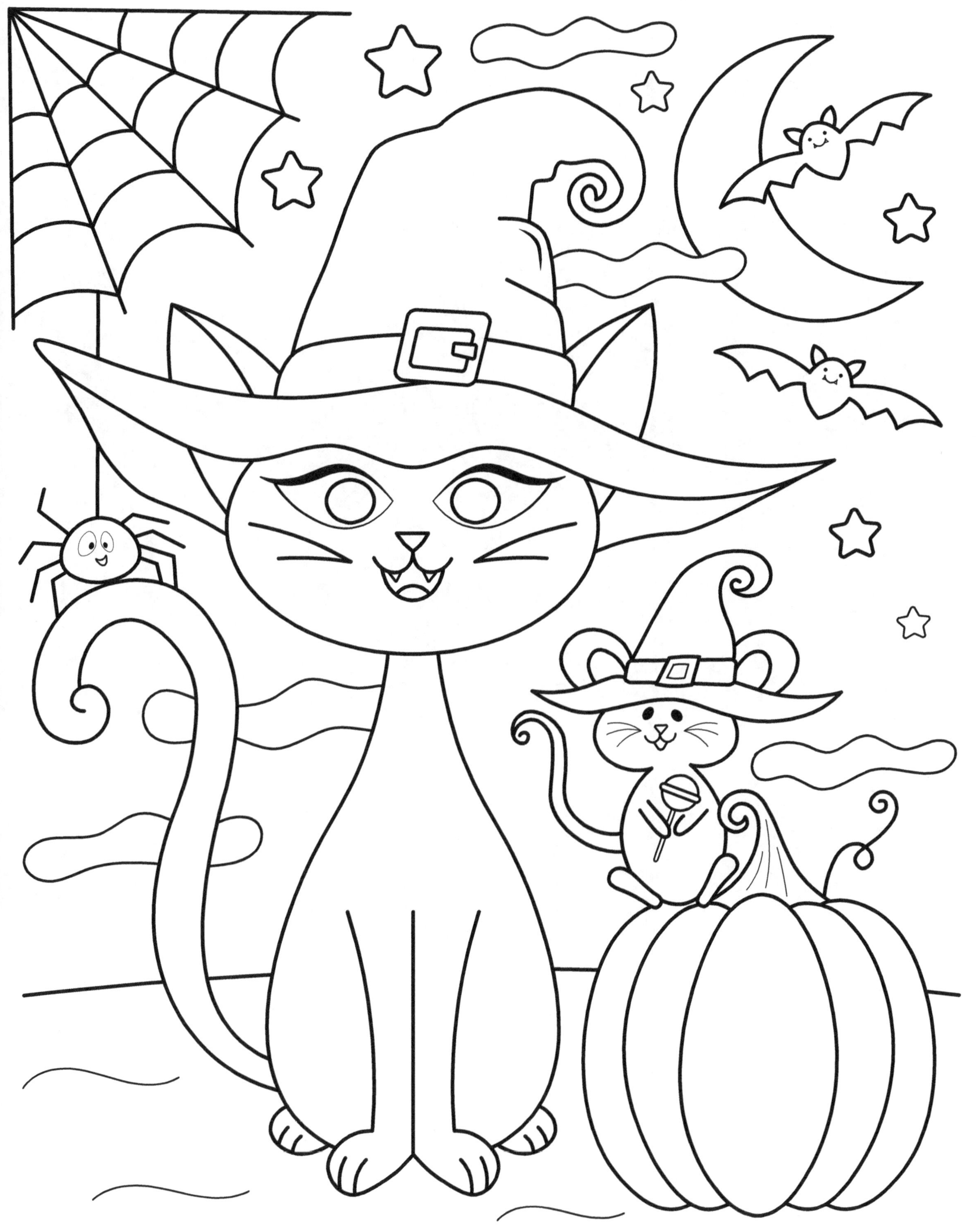

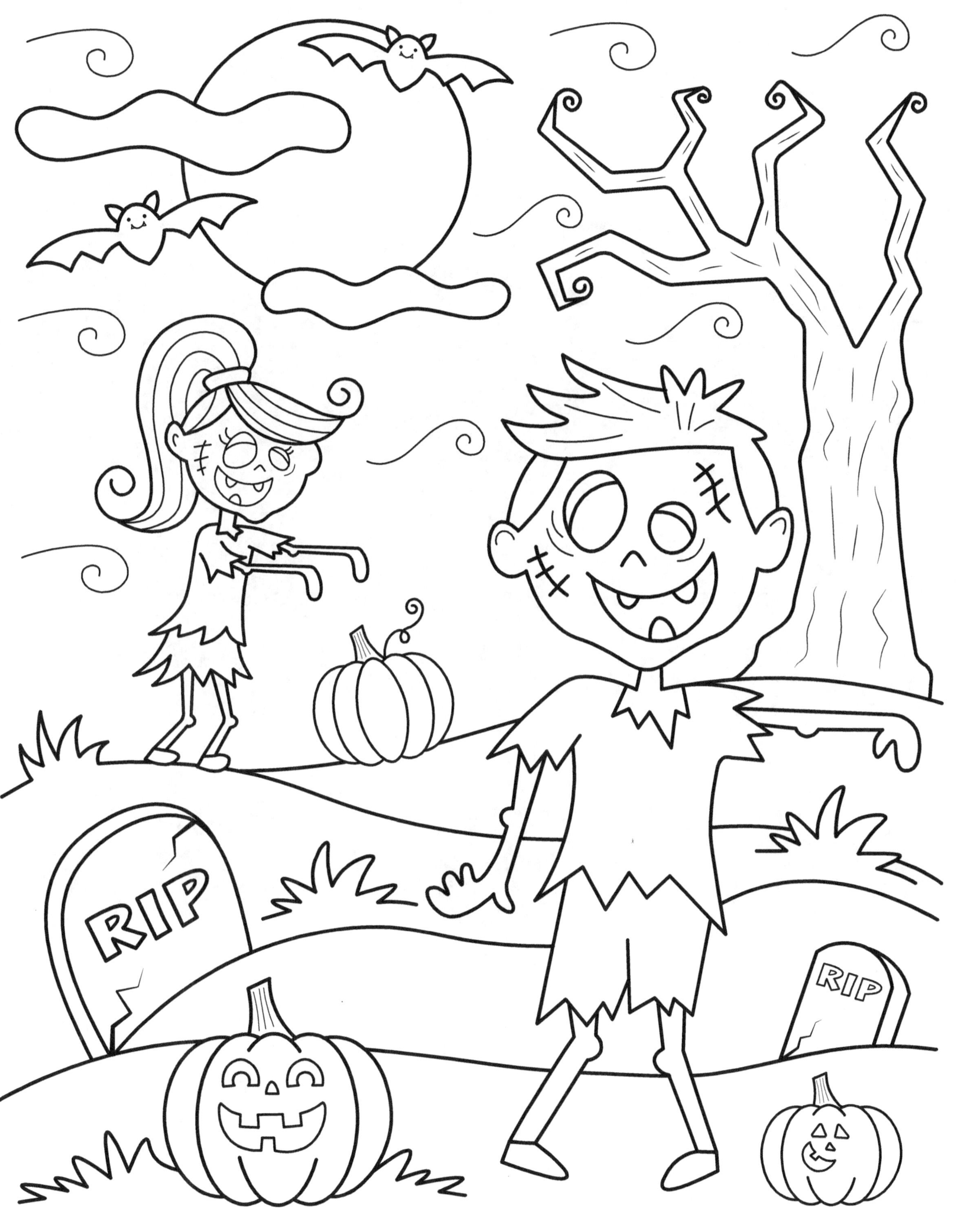

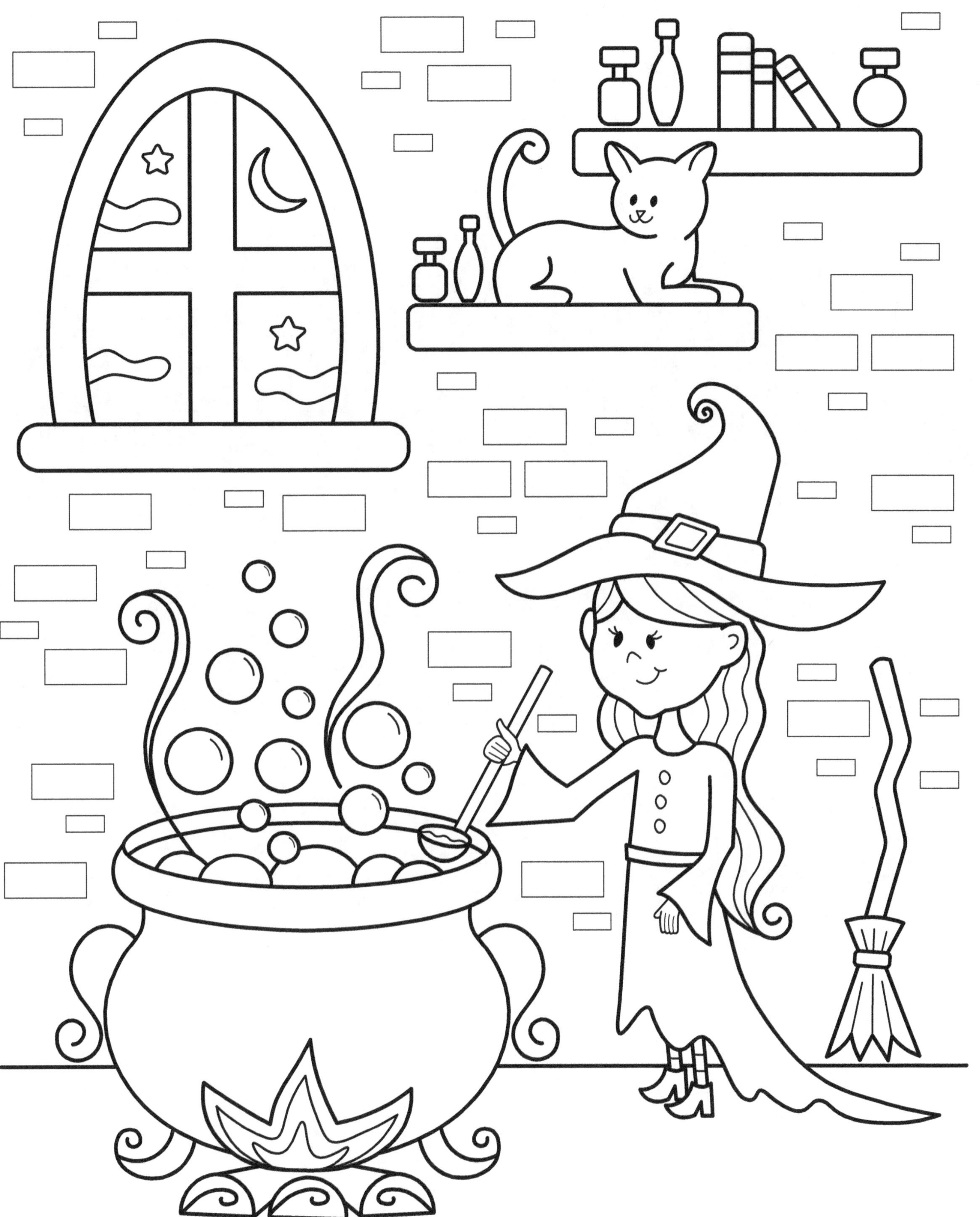

Halloween
Word Search Puzzle

```
c  g  y  k  v  j  y  j  h  g  x  b  a  z  g
o  a  h  c  i  y  n  y  p  u  m  p  k  i  n
m  p  t  o  k  w  i  t  c  h  b  r  x  k  l
o  p  y  o  s  h  d  e  a  w  a  c  c  w  l
n  m  o  r  q  t  e  x  n  h  t  i  o  k  e
b  p  q  y  c  u  y  x  d  a  r  z  b  z  z
s  s  c  a  j  g  b  r  y  t  v  t  f  r  s
j  p  m  r  m  t  r  e  a  t  m  a  b  u  d
p  i  a  e  h  o  i  m  f  g  j  r  o  k  r
t  d  p  v  z  f  n  e  h  f  e  q  f  z  o
v  e  f  n  m  s  t  s  r  g  b  v  f  h  h
l  r  n  f  x  q  k  s  t  p  j  y  y  h  i
f  v  w  d  n  e  m  p  i  e  e  z  m  n  i
r  i  l  g  d  r  r  c  m  j  r  t  y  x  d
h  t  i  s  k  e  g  u  b  x  b  k  d  g  o
```

bat	monster	spooky
candy	owl	treat
cat	pumpkin	trick
ghost	spider	witch

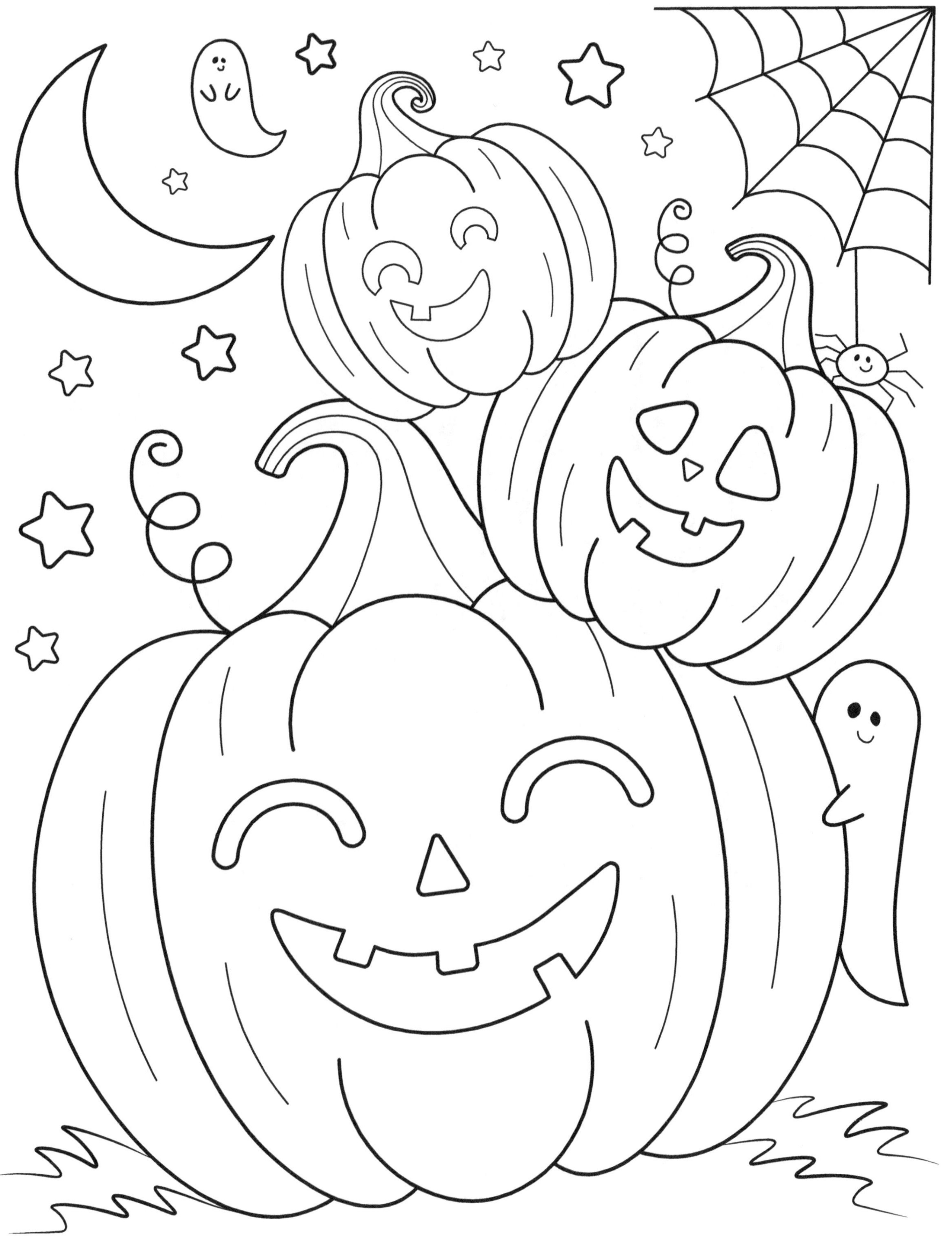

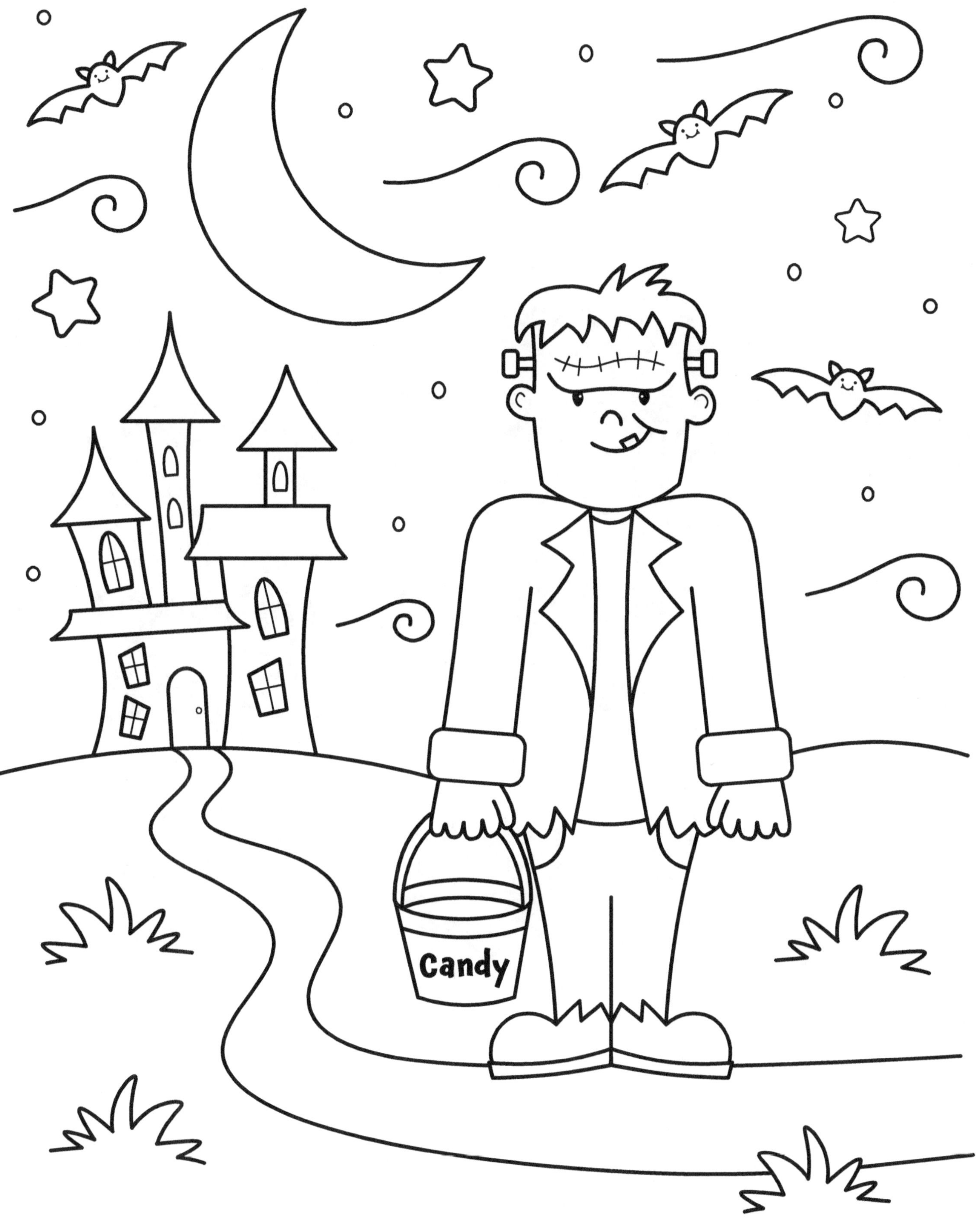

Candy

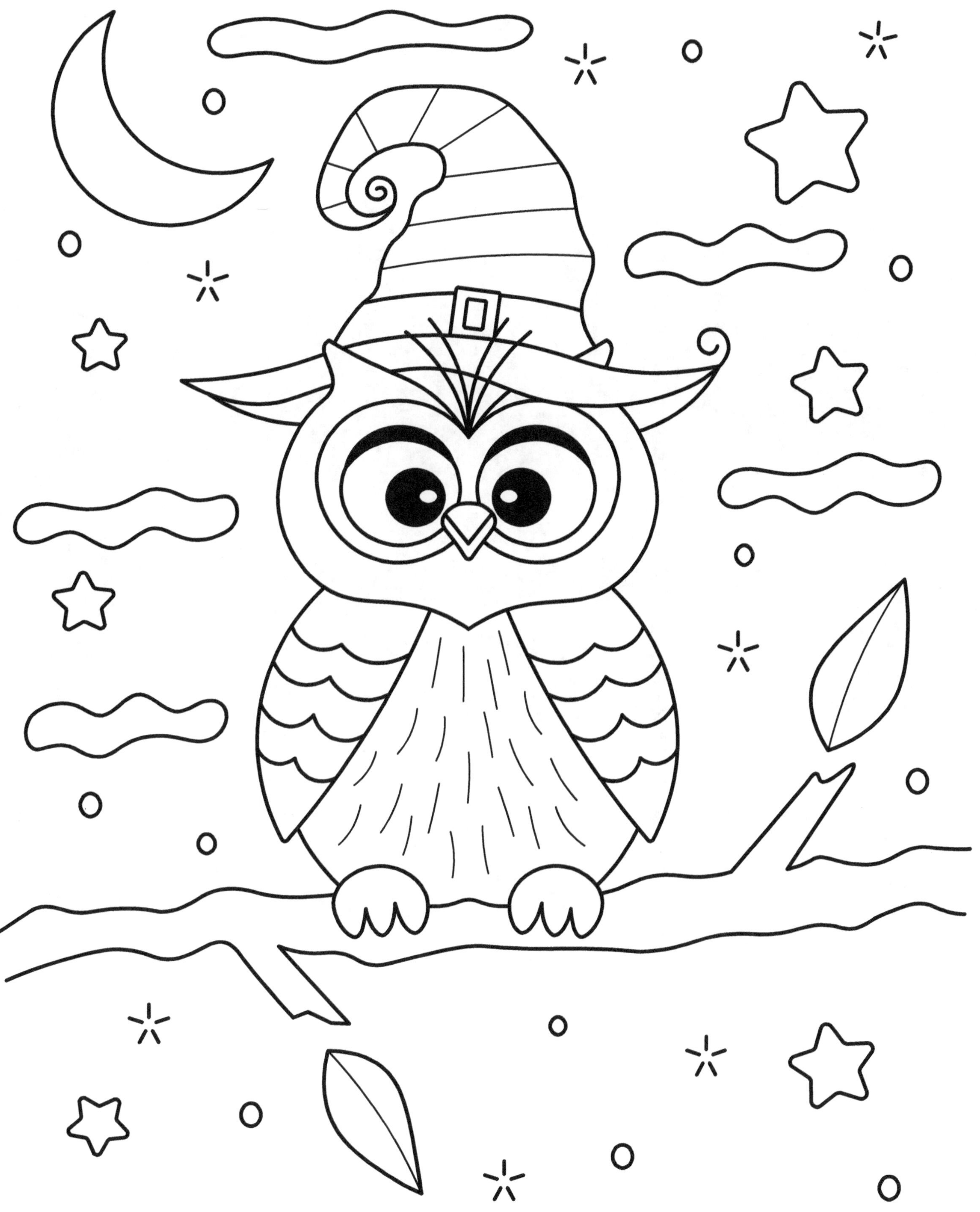

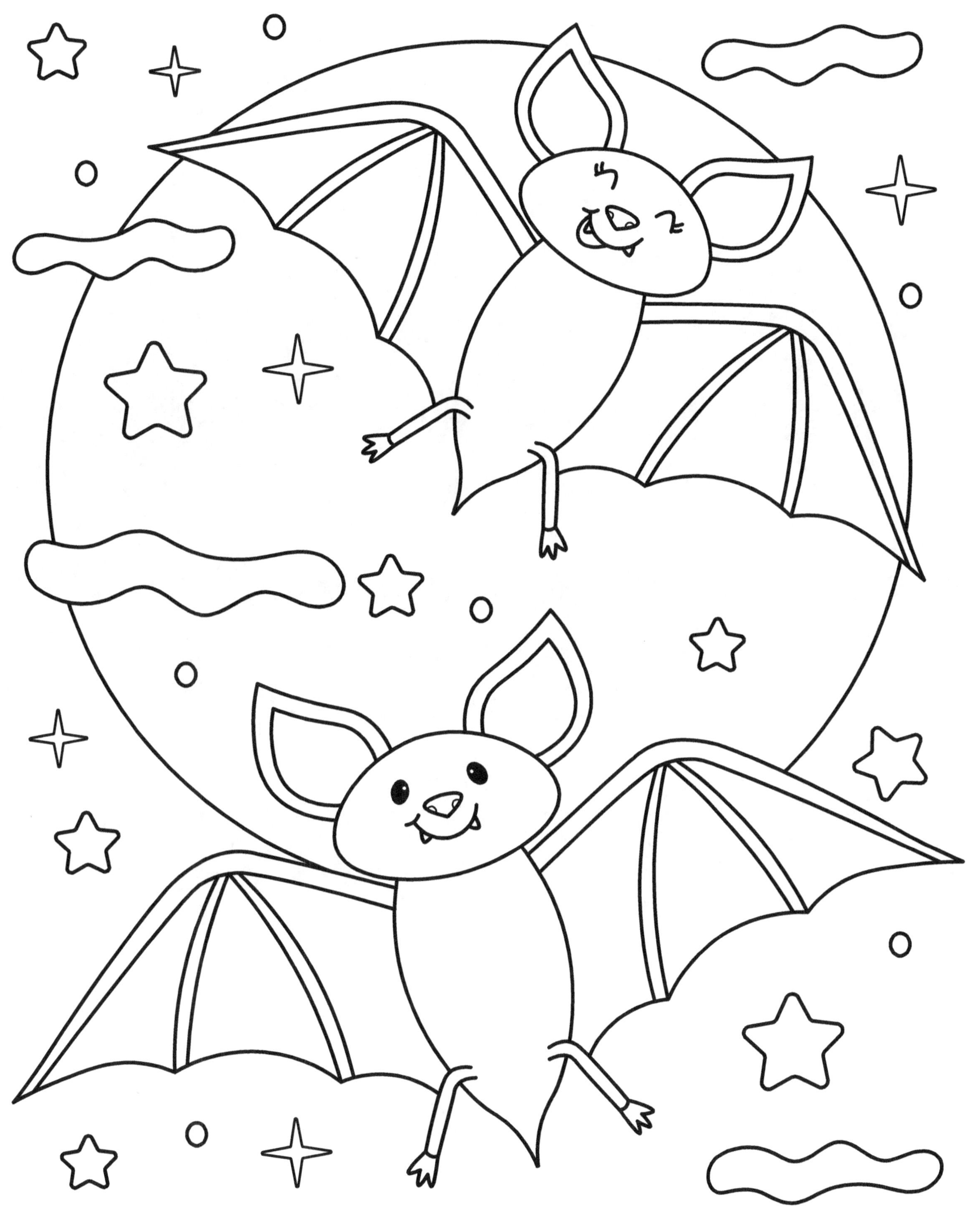

Connect the dots from 1-43 to complete the spooky house.
Then enjoy coloring the picture!

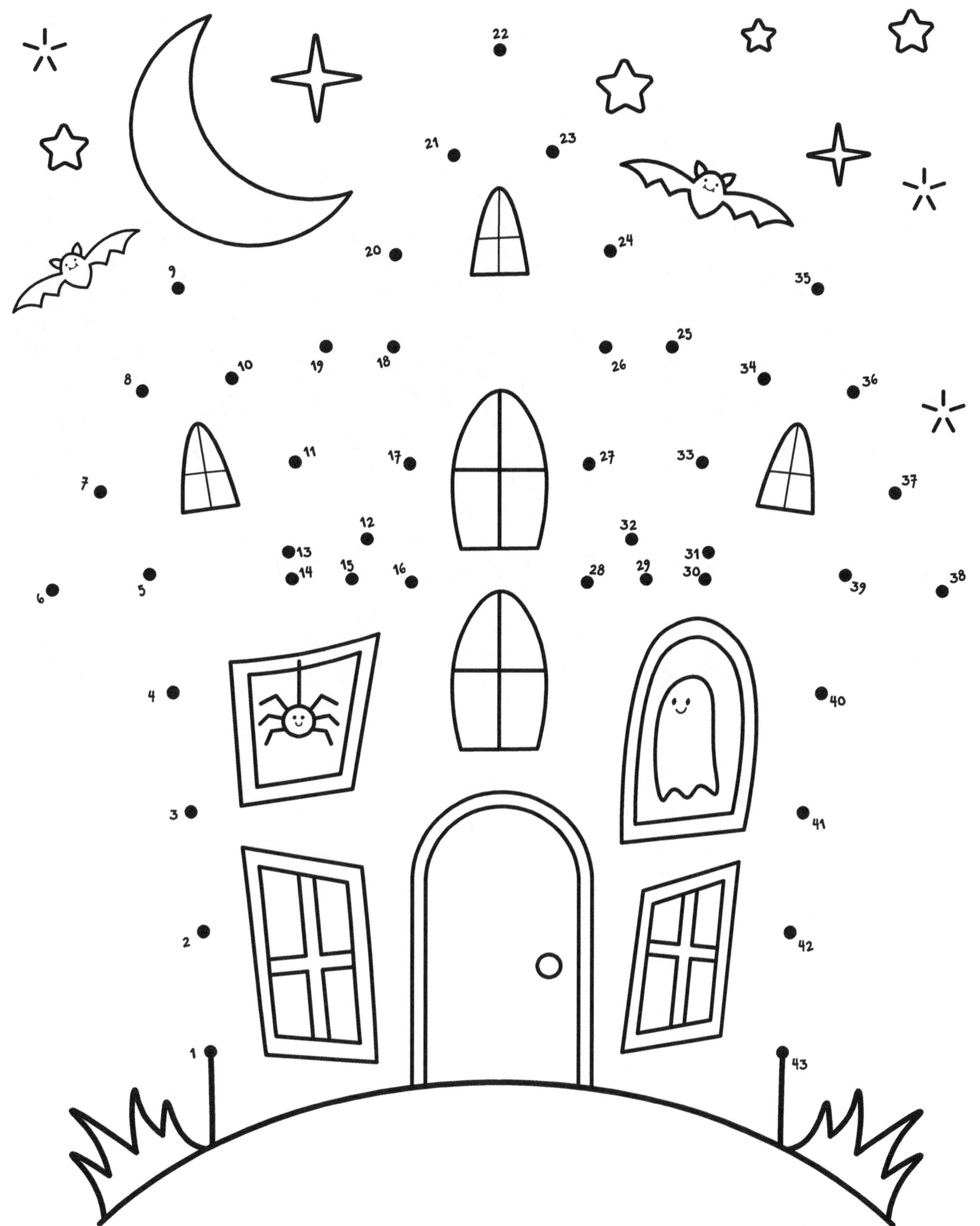

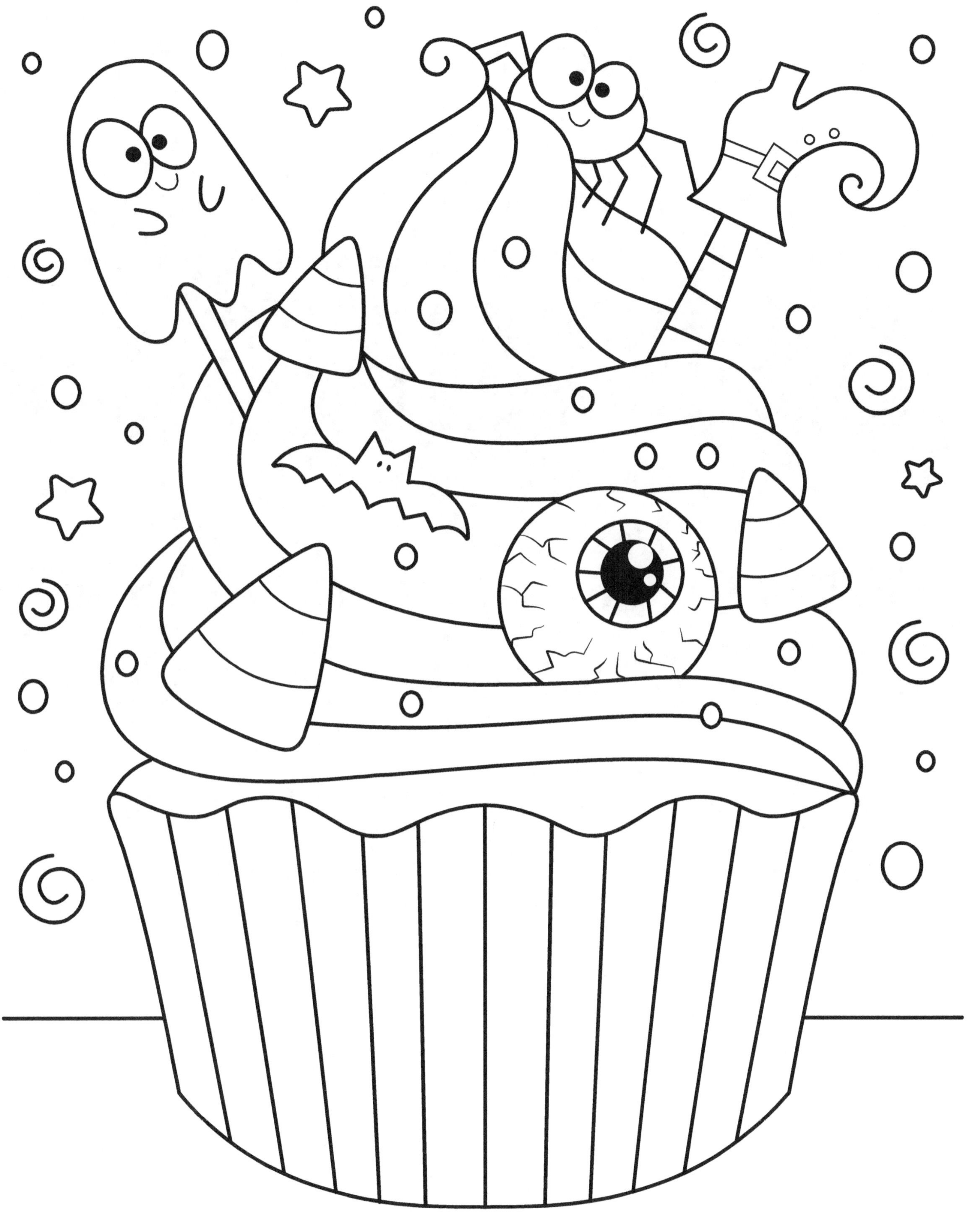

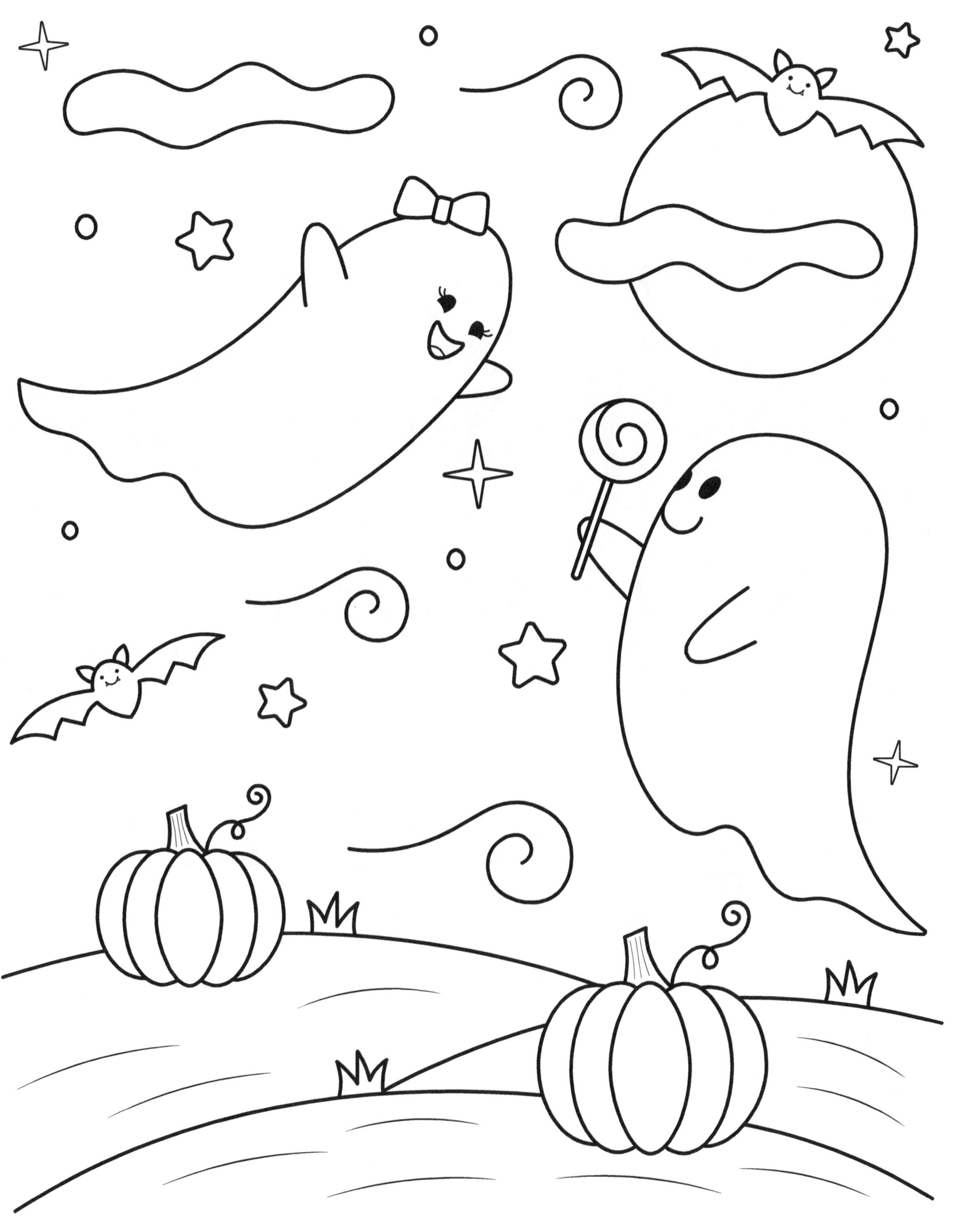

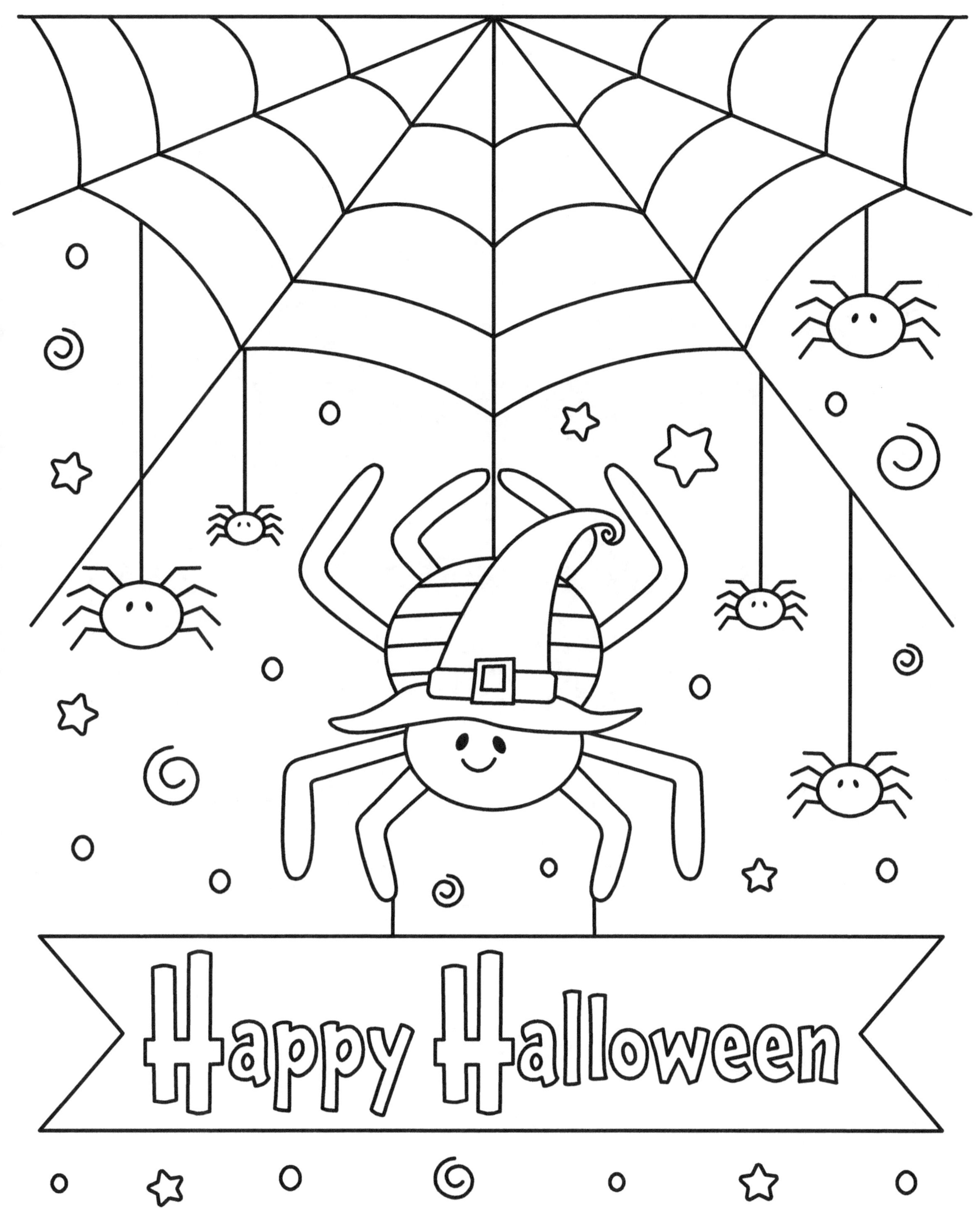

Happy Halloween

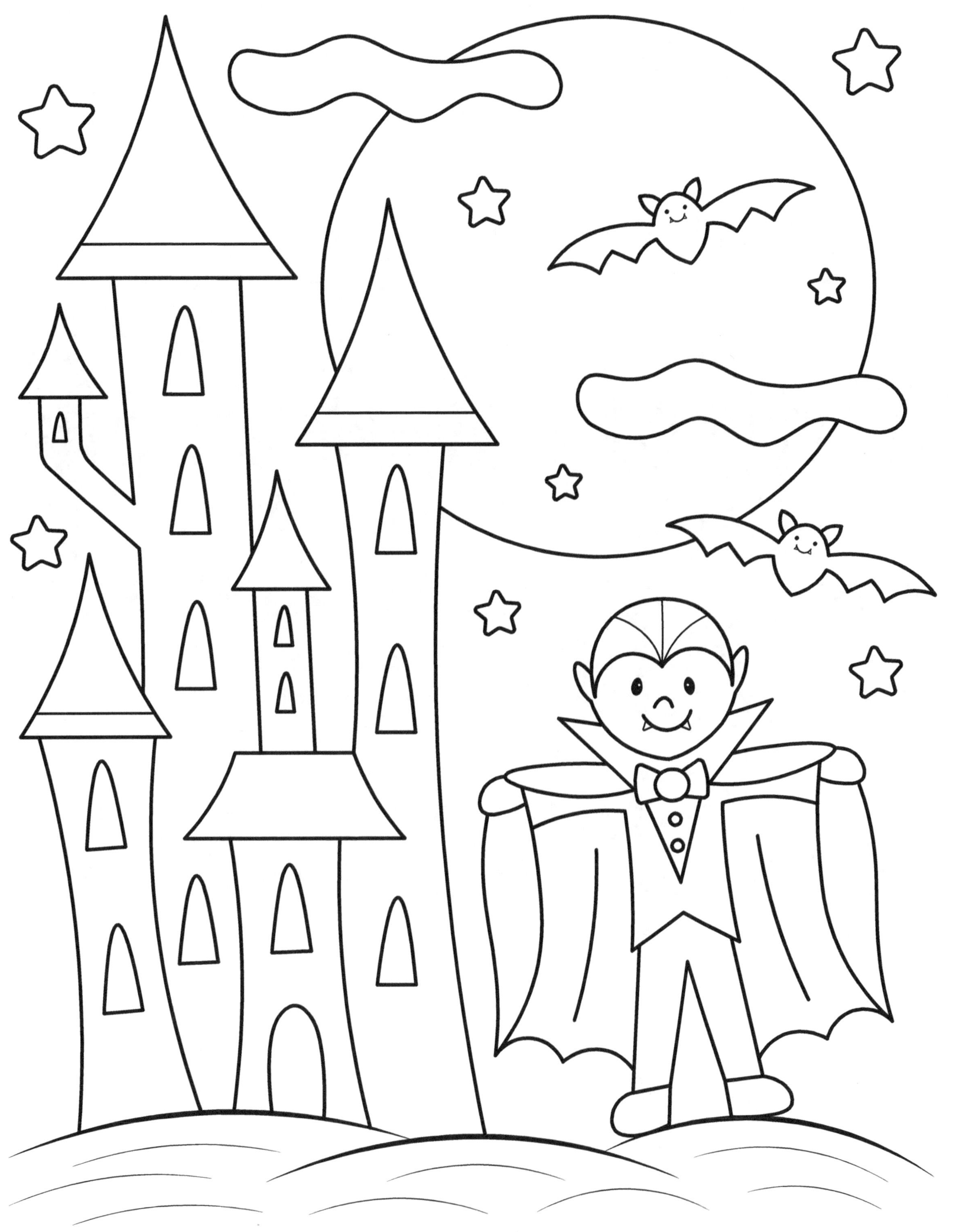

Color By Number

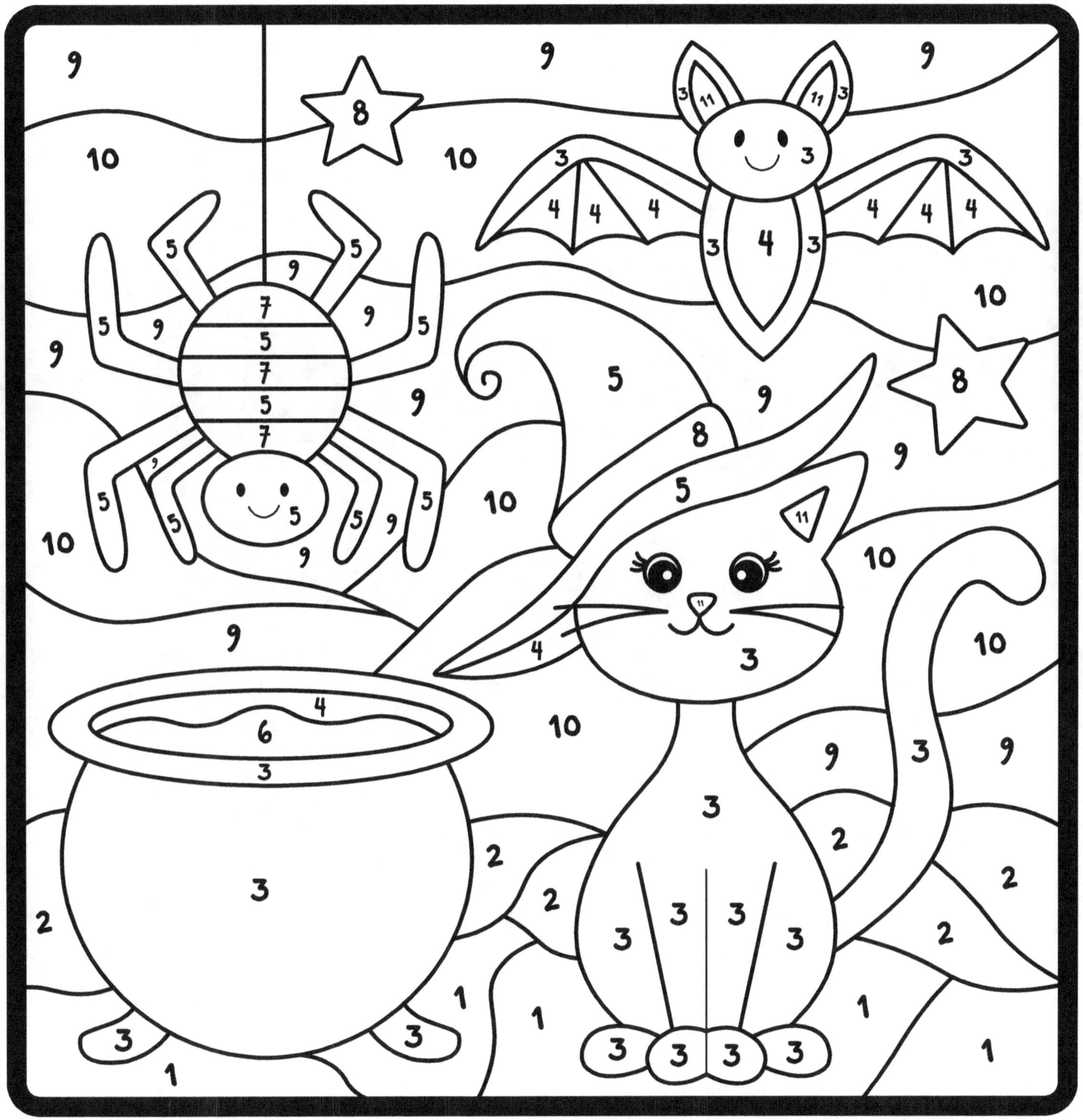

1 - Brown
4 - Gray
7 - Red
10 - Light Blue

2 - Green
5 - Purple
8 - Yellow
11 - Pink

3 - Black
6 - Light Green
9 - Blue

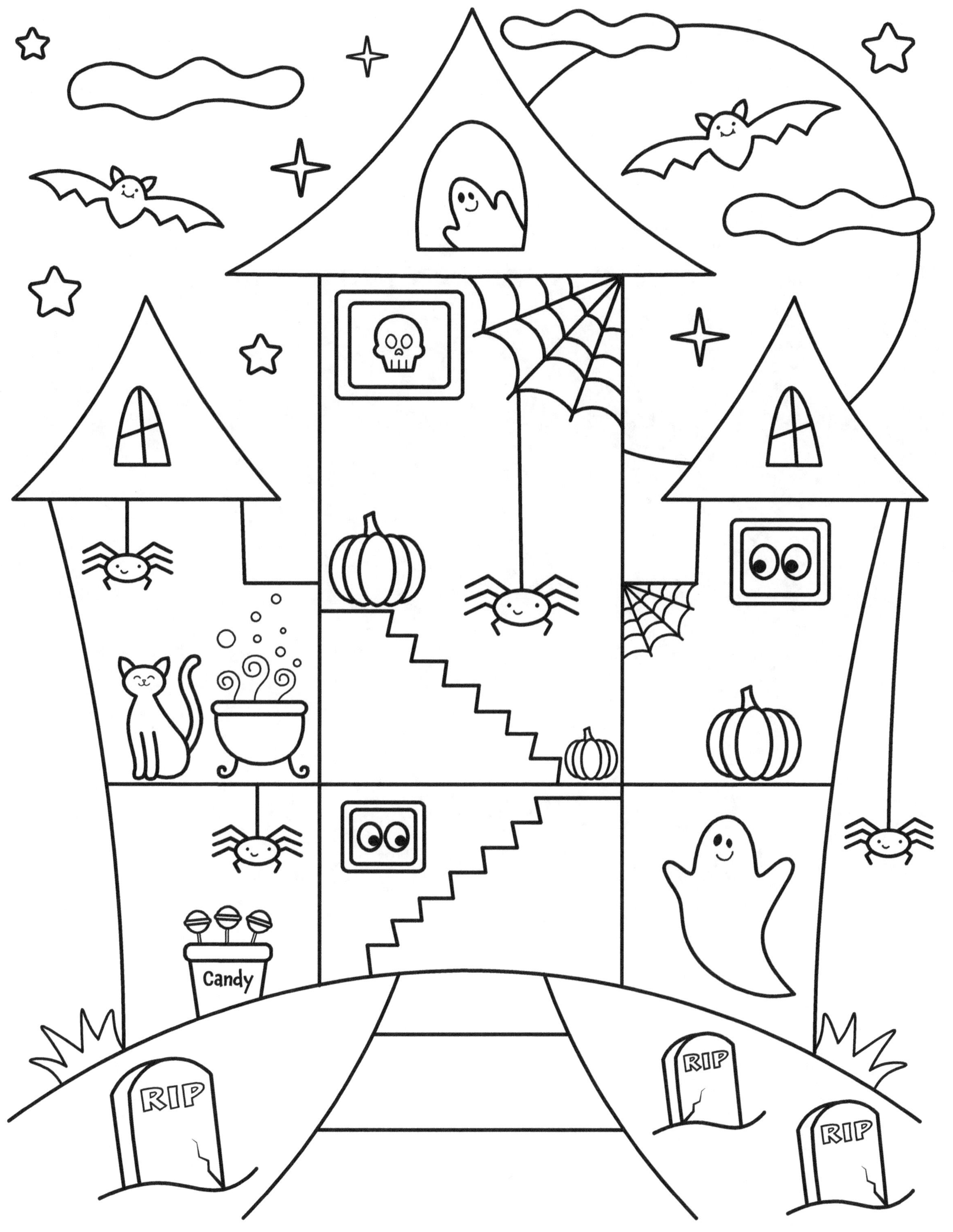

Candy
RIP
RIP
RIP

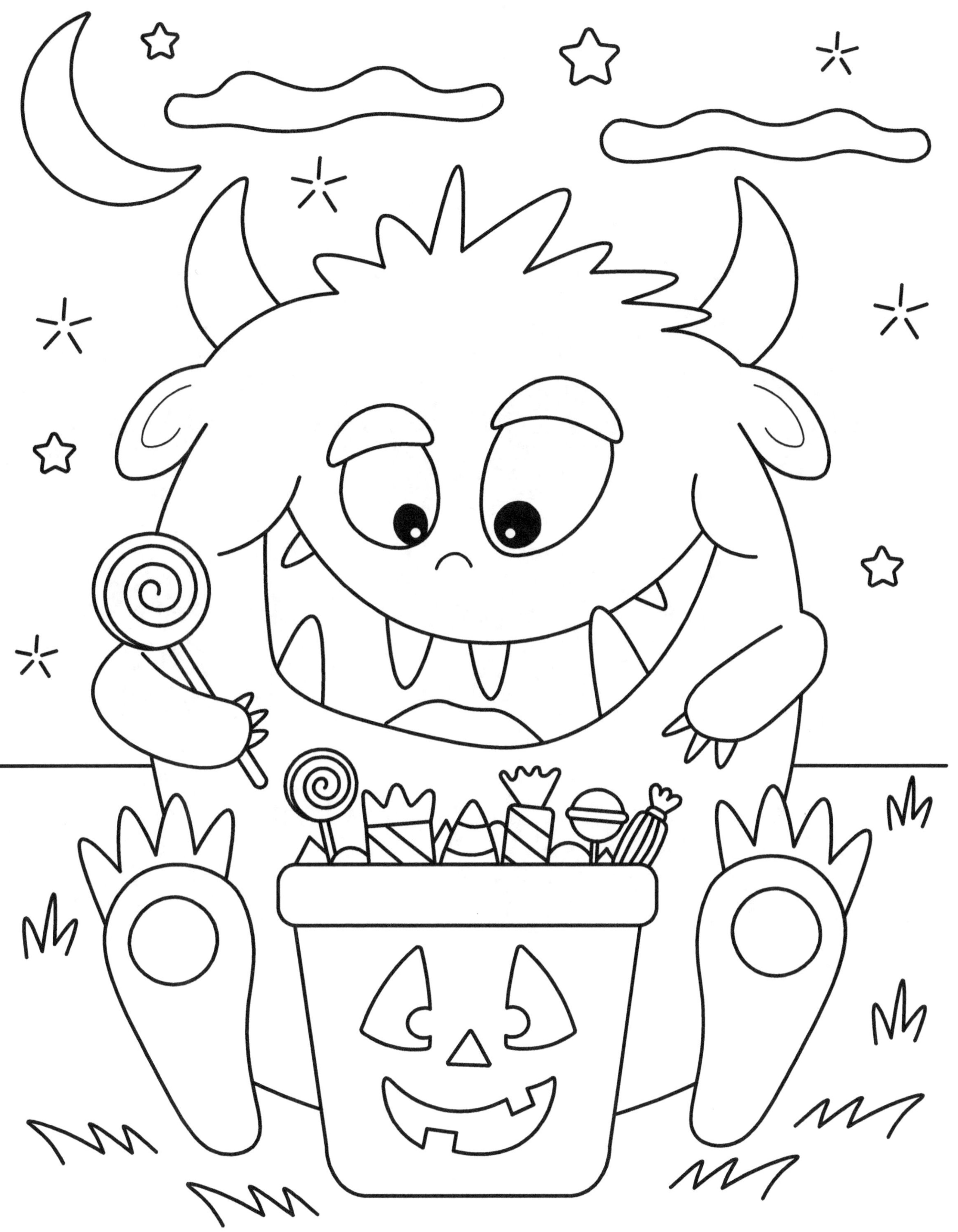

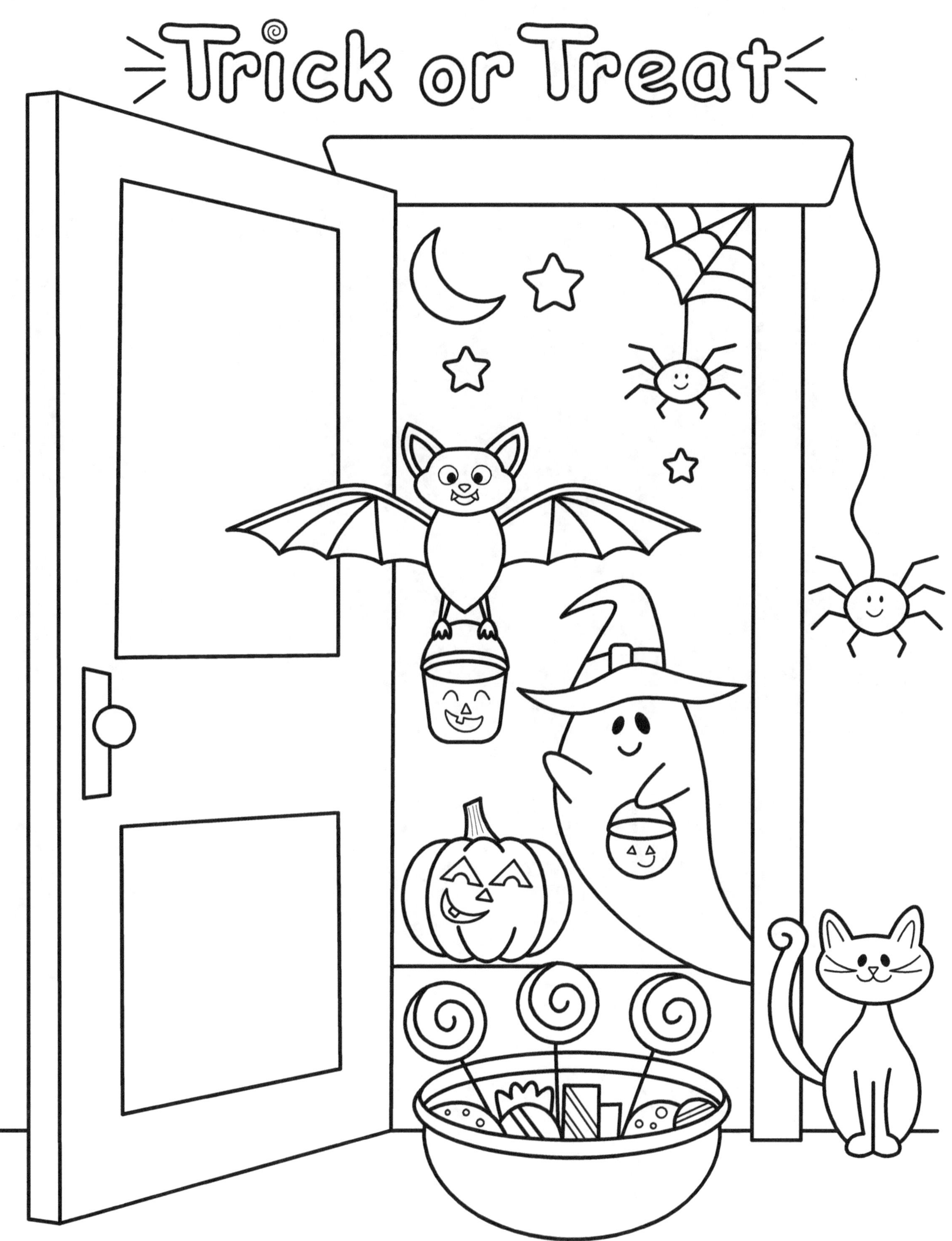

Trick or Treat

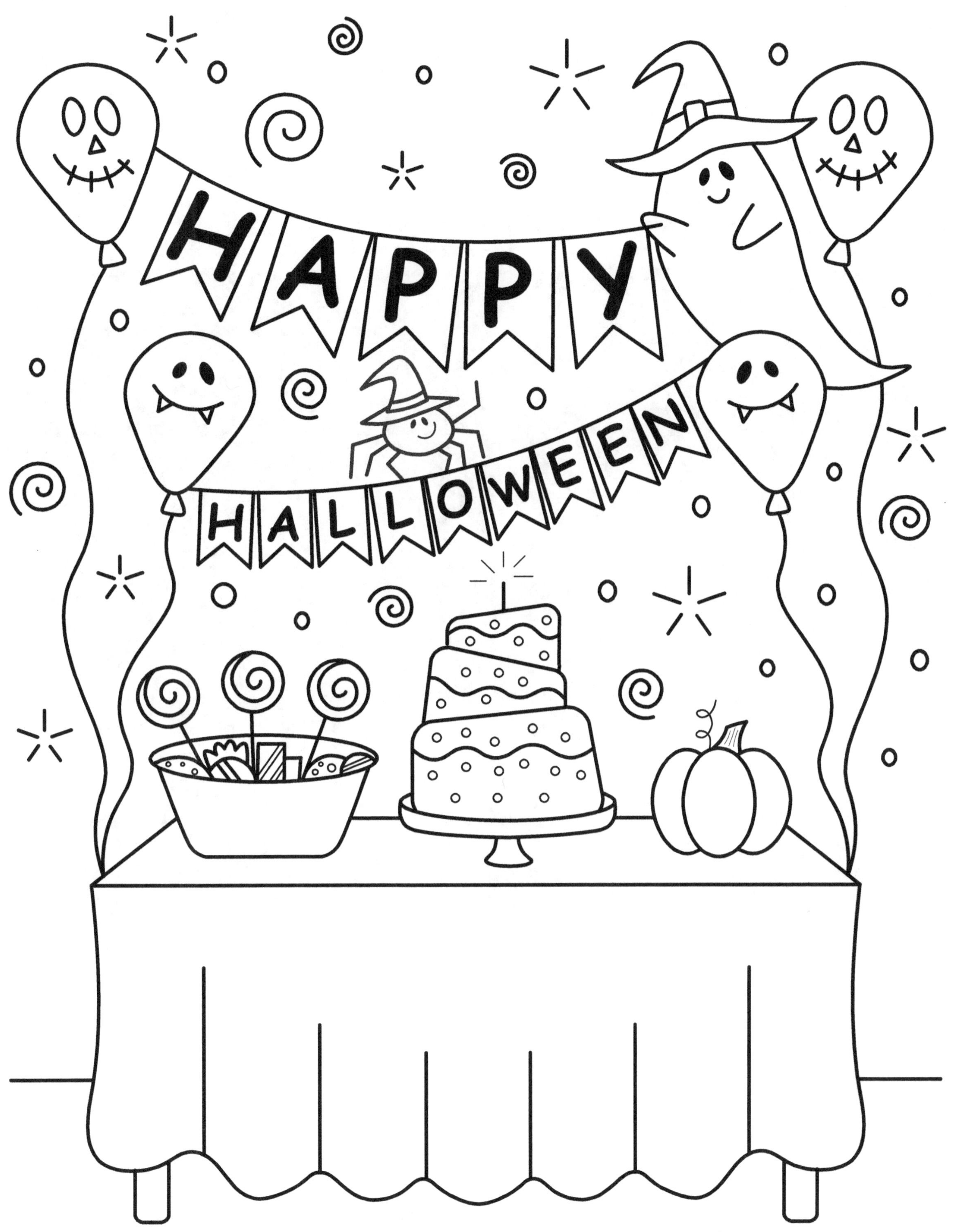

HAPPY
HALLOWEEN

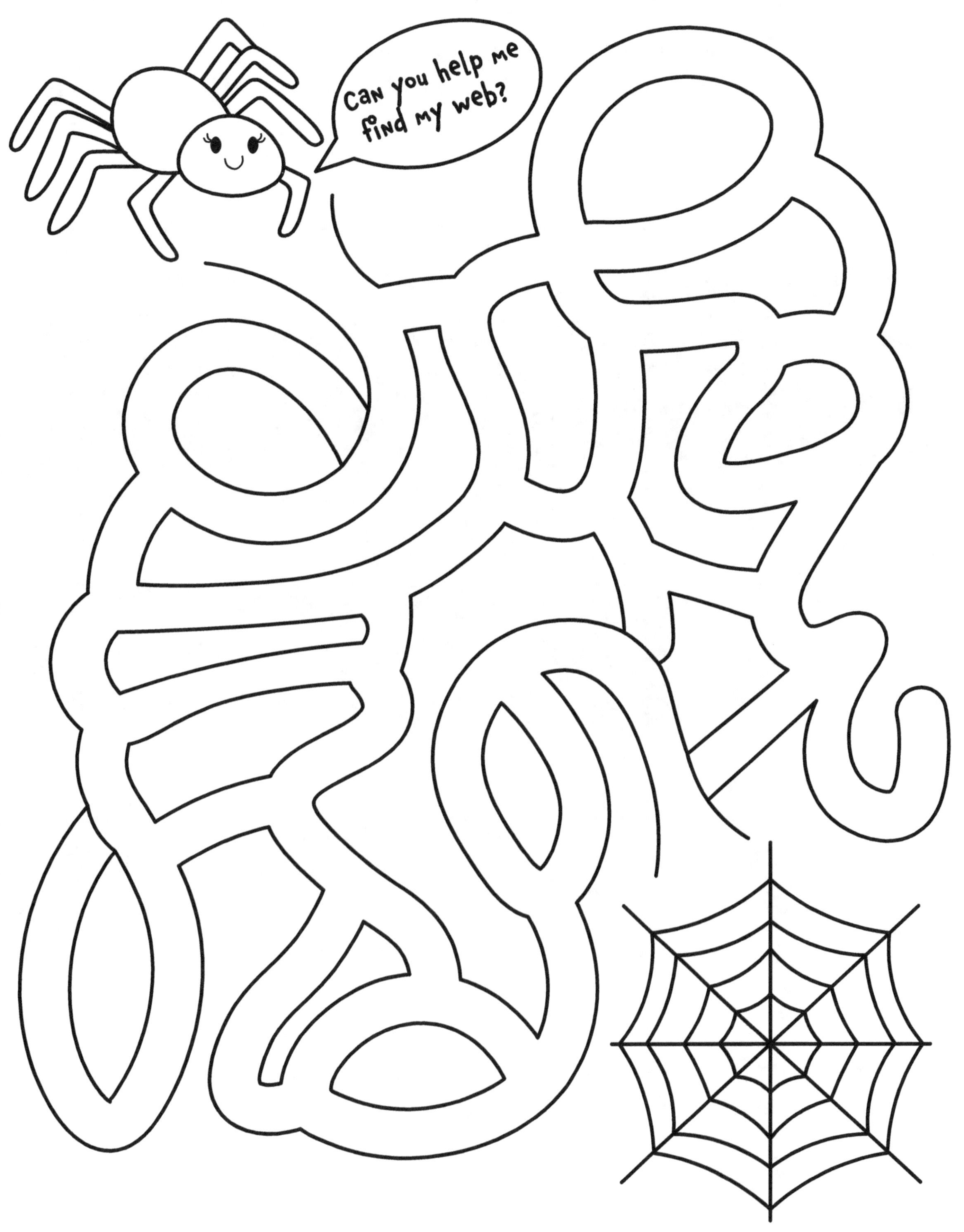

Can you help me find my web?

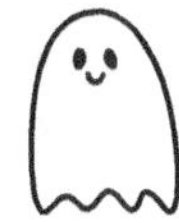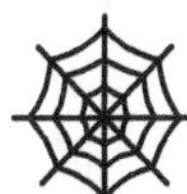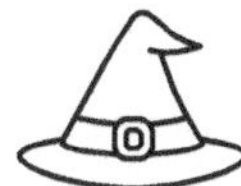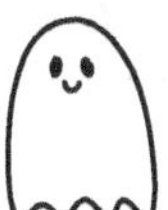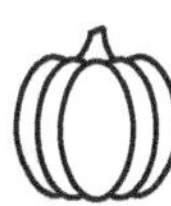
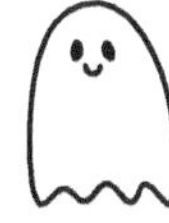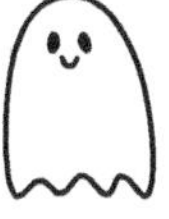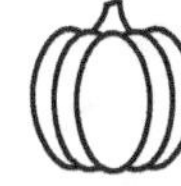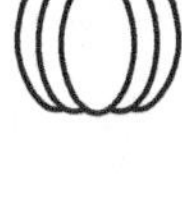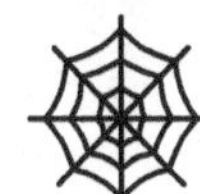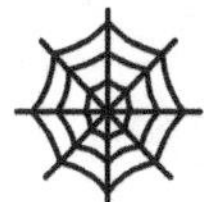

Hello! My name is Amber, the illustrator, and owner of Colorful Creative Kids; thank you so much for purchasing this coloring book! As a mom, I understand that taking the time to research quality and authentic products that entertain, educate, and induce creativity in our little ones is very important. This is why each coloring page was hand-sketched and converted to a digital image, generating clean and consistent lines to create an enjoyable experience for younger artists! I hope it brings your child hours of coloring fun and ignites their creative spark!

Colorful Creative Kids is a Veteran Owned Small Business and sincerely appreciates your purchase and feedback. Please take a few moments to leave a review online!

For more information about CCK, visit us at www.colorfulcreativekids.com or contact us at info@colorfulcreativekids.com.

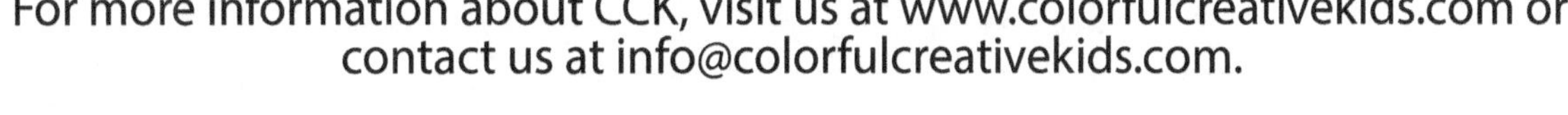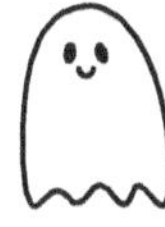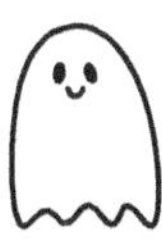

<u>Copyright Notice</u>

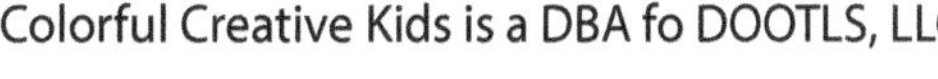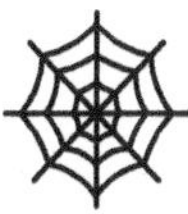
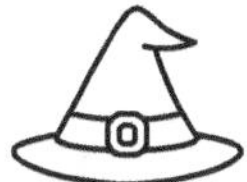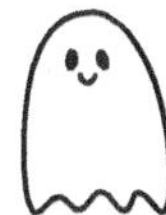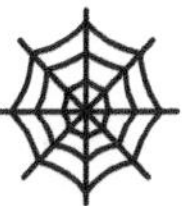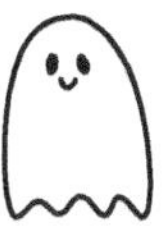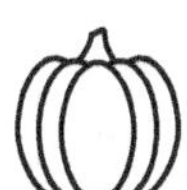